MONTHLY BUDGET PLANNER

INCOME, EXPENSE, &
DEBT FREE TRACKER,
PLUS
SNOWBALL METHOD
TRACKER

BY

SCOTT L. SMITH, JR.
FOUNDER
DEBTREDUCTION101.COM

Monthly Budget Planner: Income, Expense, & Debt Free Tracker, Plus Snowball Method Tracker
By Scott L. Smith, Jr.

ISBN-13 (paperback): 978-1-950782-63-5
 Holy Water Books (Publisher)
Cover design by Holy Water Books

MONTHLY BUDGET PLANNER

TABLE OF CONTENTS

FOR ADDITIONAL HELP

GO TO

DEBTREDUCTION101.COM

CALENDAR

MONTH: ______________________

SUN	MON	TUE	WED	THU	FRI	SAT

FINANCIAL GOALS

CALENDAR

MONTH: ______________________

SUN	MON	TUE	WED	THU	FRI	SAT

FINANCIAL GOALS

CALENDAR

MONTH: ______________________

SUN	MON	TUE	WED	THU	FRI	SAT

FINANCIAL GOALS

CALENDAR

MONTH: ______________________

SUN	MON	TUE	WED	THU	FRI	SAT

FINANCIAL GOALS

CALENDAR

MONTH: ______________________

SUN	MON	TUE	WED	THU	FRI	SAT

FINANCIAL GOALS

CALENDAR

MONTH: ______________________

SUN	MON	TUE	WED	THU	FRI	SAT

FINANCIAL GOALS

CALENDAR

MONTH: ______________________

SUN	MON	TUE	WED	THU	FRI	SAT

FINANCIAL GOALS

CALENDAR

MONTH: ______________________

SUN	MON	TUE	WED	THU	FRI	SAT

FINANCIAL GOALS

CALENDAR

MONTH: ______________________________

SUN	MON	TUE	WED	THU	FRI	SAT

FINANCIAL GOALS

CALENDAR

MONTH: ______________________

SUN	MON	TUE	WED	THU	FRI	SAT

FINANCIAL GOALS

CALENDAR

MONTH: ______________________

SUN	MON	TUE	WED	THU	FRI	SAT

FINANCIAL GOALS

CALENDAR

MONTH: ____________________

SUN	MON	TUE	WED	THU	FRI	SAT

FINANCIAL GOALS

CALENDAR

MONTH: ______________________

SUN	MON	TUE	WED	THU	FRI	SAT

FINANCIAL GOALS

CALENDAR

MONTH: ____________________

SUN	MON	TUE	WED	THU	FRI	SAT

FINANCIAL GOALS

CALENDAR

MONTH: ______________________

SUN	MON	TUE	WED	THU	FRI	SAT

FINANCIAL GOALS

CALENDAR

MONTH: ______________________

SUN	MON	TUE	WED	THU	FRI	SAT

FINANCIAL GOALS

CALENDAR

MONTH: ____________________

SUN	MON	TUE	WED	THU	FRI	SAT

FINANCIAL GOALS

CALENDAR

MONTH: ______________________

SUN	MON	TUE	WED	THU	FRI	SAT

FINANCIAL GOALS

CALENDAR

MONTH: ______________________

SUN	MON	TUE	WED	THU	FRI	SAT

FINANCIAL GOALS

CALENDAR

MONTH: ____________________

SUN	MON	TUE	WED	THU	FRI	SAT

FINANCIAL GOALS

CALENDAR

MONTH: ______________________

SUN	MON	TUE	WED	THU	FRI	SAT

FINANCIAL GOALS

CALENDAR

MONTH: ______________________

SUN	MON	TUE	WED	THU	FRI	SAT

FINANCIAL GOALS

CALENDAR

MONTH: ______________________

SUN	MON	TUE	WED	THU	FRI	SAT

FINANCIAL GOALS

CALENDAR

MONTH: ______________________

SUN	MON	TUE	WED	THU	FRI	SAT

FINANCIAL GOALS

CALENDAR

MONTH: ______________________

SUN	MON	TUE	WED	THU	FRI	SAT

FINANCIAL GOALS

CALENDAR

MONTH: ______________________

SUN	MON	TUE	WED	THU	FRI	SAT

FINANCIAL GOALS

MONTHLY BUDGET

MONTH OF				
TOTAL INCOME		OTHER INCOME / SAVINGS		

EXPENSES ITEM	BUDGET	ACTUAL	DIFFERENCE	NOTES
MORTGAGE/RENT				
HOUSEHOLD MAINTENANCE				
TAXES				
INSURANCE				
ELECTRICITY				
WATER				
SEWAGE				
GAS				
PHONE				
TRASH				
CABLE				
CELL PHONE				
GROCERIES				
ENTERTAINMENT				
CHARITY/DONATIONS				
FUEL				
AUTO INSURANCE				
CAR PAYMENT				
CHILD CARE				
CREDIT CARDS/DEBT				
LOANS				
DINING OUT				
SPORTING EVENTS				
LIVE THEATER				
CONCERTS				
MOVIES				
TOTAL EXPENSES				

NOTES

JANUARY

INCOMES & EXPENSES

DATE	INCOME	CATEGORY	AMOUNT
			TOTAL

DATE	EXPENSE	CATEGORY	AMOUNT
			TOTAL

JANUARY

INCOMES & EXPENSES

DATE	INCOME	CATEGORY	AMOUNT
			TOTAL

DATE	EXPENSE	CATEGORY	AMOUNT
			TOTAL

JANUARY

INCOMES & EXPENSES

DATE	INCOME	CATEGORY	AMOUNT
			TOTAL

DATE	EXPENSE	CATEGORY	AMOUNT
			TOTAL

JANUARY

INCOMES & EXPENSES

DATE	INCOME	CATEGORY	AMOUNT
			TOTAL

DATE	EXPENSE	CATEGORY	AMOUNT
			TOTAL

MONTHLY BUDGET

MONTH OF	
TOTAL INCOME	OTHER INCOME / SAVINGS

EXPENSES ITEM	BUDGET	ACTUAL	DIFFERENCE	NOTES
MORTGAGE/RENT				
HOUSEHOLD MAINTENANCE				
TAXES				
INSURANCE				
ELECTRICITY				
WATER				
SEWAGE				
GAS				
PHONE				
TRASH				
CABLE				
CELL PHONE				
GROCERIES				
ENTERTAINMENT				
CHARITY/DONATIONS				
FUEL				
AUTO INSURANCE				
CAR PAYMENT				
CHILD CARE				
CREDIT CARDS/DEBT				
LOANS				
DINING OUT				
SPORTING EVENTS				
LIVE THEATER				
CONCERTS				
MOVIES				
TOTAL EXPENSES				

NOTES

FEBRUARY

INCOMES & EXPENSES

DATE	INCOME	CATEGORY	AMOUNT
			TOTAL

DATE	EXPENSE	CATEGORY	AMOUNT
			TOTAL

FEBRUARY

INCOMES & EXPENSES

DATE	INCOME	CATEGORY	AMOUNT
			TOTAL

DATE	EXPENSE	CATEGORY	AMOUNT
			TOTAL

FEBRUARY

INCOMES & EXPENSES

DATE	INCOME	CATEGORY	AMOUNT
			TOTAL

DATE	EXPENSE	CATEGORY	AMOUNT
			TOTAL

FEBRUARY

INCOMES & EXPENSES

DATE	INCOME	CATEGORY	AMOUNT
			TOTAL

DATE	EXPENSE	CATEGORY	AMOUNT
			TOTAL

FEBRUARY

INCOMES & EXPENSES

DATE	INCOME	CATEGORY	AMOUNT
			TOTAL

DATE	EXPENSE	CATEGORY	AMOUNT
			TOTAL

MONTHLY BUDGET

MONTH OF	
TOTAL INCOME	OTHER INCOME / SAVINGS

EXPENSES ITEM	BUDGET	ACTUAL	DIFFERENCE	NOTES
MORTGAGE/RENT				
HOUSEHOLD MAINTENANCE				
TAXES				
INSURANCE				
ELECTRICITY				
WATER				
SEWAGE				
GAS				
PHONE				
TRASH				
CABLE				
CELL PHONE				
GROCERIES				
ENTERTAINMENT				
CHARITY/DONATIONS				
FUEL				
AUTO INSURANCE				
CAR PAYMENT				
CHILD CARE				
CREDIT CARDS/DEBT				
LOANS				
DINING OUT				
SPORTING EVENTS				
LIVE THEATER				
CONCERTS				
MOVIES				
TOTAL EXPENSES				

NOTES

MARCH

INCOMES & EXPENSES

DATE	INCOME	CATEGORY	AMOUNT
			TOTAL

DATE	EXPENSE	CATEGORY	AMOUNT
			TOTAL

MARCH

INCOMES & EXPENSES

DATE	INCOME	CATEGORY	AMOUNT
			TOTAL

DATE	EXPENSE	CATEGORY	AMOUNT
			TOTAL

MARCH

INCOMES & EXPENSES

DATE	INCOME	CATEGORY	AMOUNT
			TOTAL

DATE	EXPENSE	CATEGORY	AMOUNT
			TOTAL

MARCH

INCOMES & EXPENSES

DATE	INCOME	CATEGORY	AMOUNT
			TOTAL

DATE	EXPENSE	CATEGORY	AMOUNT
			TOTAL

MARCH

INCOMES & EXPENSES

DATE	INCOME	CATEGORY	AMOUNT
			TOTAL

DATE	EXPENSE	CATEGORY	AMOUNT
			TOTAL

MONTHLY BUDGET

MONTH OF

TOTAL INCOME | OTHER INCOME / SAVINGS

EXPENSES ITEM	BUDGET	ACTUAL	DIFFERENCE	NOTES
MORTGAGE/RENT				
HOUSEHOLD MAINTENANCE				
TAXES				
INSURANCE				
ELECTRICITY				
WATER				
SEWAGE				
GAS				
PHONE				
TRASH				
CABLE				
CELL PHONE				
GROCERIES				
ENTERTAINMENT				
CHARITY/DONATIONS				
FUEL				
AUTO INSURANCE				
CAR PAYMENT				
CHILD CARE				
CREDIT CARDS/DEBT				
LOANS				
DINING OUT				
SPORTING EVENTS				
LIVE THEATER				
CONCERTS				
MOVIES				
TOTAL EXPENSES				

NOTES

APRIL

INCOMES & EXPENSES

DATE	INCOME	CATEGORY	AMOUNT
			TOTAL

DATE	EXPENSE	CATEGORY	AMOUNT
			TOTAL

APRIL

INCOMES & EXPENSES

DATE	INCOME	CATEGORY	AMOUNT
			TOTAL

DATE	EXPENSE	CATEGORY	AMOUNT
			TOTAL

APRIL

INCOMES & EXPENSES

DATE	INCOME	CATEGORY	AMOUNT
			TOTAL

DATE	EXPENSE	CATEGORY	AMOUNT
			TOTAL

APRIL

INCOMES & EXPENSES

DATE	INCOME	CATEGORY	AMOUNT
			TOTAL

DATE	EXPENSE	CATEGORY	AMOUNT
			TOTAL

APRIL

INCOMES & EXPENSES

DATE	INCOME	CATEGORY	AMOUNT
			TOTAL

DATE	EXPENSE	CATEGORY	AMOUNT
			TOTAL

MONTHLY BUDGET

MONTH OF	
TOTAL INCOME	OTHER INCOME / SAVINGS

EXPENSES ITEM	BUDGET	ACTUAL	DIFFERENCE	NOTES
MORTGAGE/RENT				
HOUSEHOLD MAINTENANCE				
TAXES				
INSURANCE				
ELECTRICITY				
WATER				
SEWAGE				
GAS				
PHONE				
TRASH				
CABLE				
CELL PHONE				
GROCERIES				
ENTERTAINMENT				
CHARITY/DONATIONS				
FUEL				
AUTO INSURANCE				
CAR PAYMENT				
CHILD CARE				
CREDIT CARDS/DEBT				
LOANS				
DINING OUT				
SPORTING EVENTS				
LIVE THEATER				
CONCERTS				
MOVIES				
TOTAL EXPENSES				

NOTES

MAY

INCOMES & EXPENSES

DATE	INCOME	CATEGORY	AMOUNT
			TOTAL

DATE	EXPENSE	CATEGORY	AMOUNT
			TOTAL

MAY

INCOMES & EXPENSES

DATE	INCOME	CATEGORY	AMOUNT
			TOTAL

DATE	EXPENSE	CATEGORY	AMOUNT
			TOTAL

MAY

INCOMES & EXPENSES

DATE	INCOME	CATEGORY	AMOUNT
			TOTAL

DATE	EXPENSE	CATEGORY	AMOUNT
			TOTAL

MAY

INCOMES & EXPENSES

DATE	INCOME	CATEGORY	AMOUNT
			TOTAL

DATE	EXPENSE	CATEGORY	AMOUNT
			TOTAL

MAY

INCOMES & EXPENSES

DATE	INCOME	CATEGORY	AMOUNT
			TOTAL

DATE	EXPENSE	CATEGORY	AMOUNT
			TOTAL

MONTHLY BUDGET

MONTH OF

TOTAL INCOME

OTHER INCOME / SAVINGS

EXPENSES ITEM	BUDGET	ACTUAL	DIFFERENCE	NOTES
MORTGAGE/RENT				
HOUSEHOLD MAINTENANCE				
TAXES				
INSURANCE				
ELECTRICITY				
WATER				
SEWAGE				
GAS				
PHONE				
TRASH				
CABLE				
CELL PHONE				
GROCERIES				
ENTERTAINMENT				
CHARITY/DONATIONS				
FUEL				
AUTO INSURANCE				
CAR PAYMENT				
CHILD CARE				
CREDIT CARDS/DEBT				
LOANS				
DINING OUT				
SPORTING EVENTS				
LIVE THEATER				
CONCERTS				
MOVIES				
TOTAL EXPENSES				

NOTES

JUNE

INCOMES & EXPENSES

DATE	INCOME	CATEGORY	AMOUNT
			TOTAL

DATE	EXPENSE	CATEGORY	AMOUNT
			TOTAL

JUNE

INCOMES & EXPENSES

DATE	INCOME	CATEGORY	AMOUNT
			TOTAL

DATE	EXPENSE	CATEGORY	AMOUNT
			TOTAL

JUNE

INCOMES & EXPENSES

DATE	INCOME	CATEGORY	AMOUNT
		TOTAL	

DATE	EXPENSE	CATEGORY	AMOUNT
		TOTAL	

JUNE

INCOMES & EXPENSES

DATE	INCOME	CATEGORY	AMOUNT
			TOTAL

DATE	EXPENSE	CATEGORY	AMOUNT
			TOTAL

JUNE

INCOMES & EXPENSES

DATE	INCOME	CATEGORY	AMOUNT
			TOTAL

DATE	EXPENSE	CATEGORY	AMOUNT
			TOTAL

MONTHLY BUDGET

MONTH OF	
TOTAL INCOME	OTHER INCOME / SAVINGS

EXPENSES ITEM	BUDGET	ACTUAL	DIFFERENCE	NOTES
MORTGAGE/RENT				
HOUSEHOLD MAINTENANCE				
TAXES				
INSURANCE				
ELECTRICITY				
WATER				
SEWAGE				
GAS				
PHONE				
TRASH				
CABLE				
CELL PHONE				
GROCERIES				
ENTERTAINMENT				
CHARITY/DONATIONS				
FUEL				
AUTO INSURANCE				
CAR PAYMENT				
CHILD CARE				
CREDIT CARDS/DEBT				
LOANS				
DINING OUT				
SPORTING EVENTS				
LIVE THEATER				
CONCERTS				
MOVIES				
TOTAL EXPENSES				

NOTES

JULY

INCOMES & EXPENSES

DATE	INCOME	CATEGORY	AMOUNT
			TOTAL

DATE	EXPENSE	CATEGORY	AMOUNT
			TOTAL

JULY

INCOMES & EXPENSES

DATE	INCOME	CATEGORY	AMOUNT
			TOTAL

DATE	EXPENSE	CATEGORY	AMOUNT
			TOTAL

JULY

INCOMES & EXPENSES

DATE	INCOME	CATEGORY	AMOUNT
			TOTAL

DATE	EXPENSE	CATEGORY	AMOUNT
			TOTAL

JULY

INCOMES & EXPENSES

DATE	INCOME	CATEGORY	AMOUNT
			TOTAL

DATE	EXPENSE	CATEGORY	AMOUNT
			TOTAL

JULY

INCOMES & EXPENSES

DATE	INCOME	CATEGORY	AMOUNT
			TOTAL

DATE	EXPENSE	CATEGORY	AMOUNT
			TOTAL

MONTHLY BUDGET

MONTH OF				
TOTAL INCOME		OTHER INCOME / SAVINGS		

EXPENSES ITEM	BUDGET	ACTUAL	DIFFERENCE	NOTES
MORTGAGE/RENT				
HOUSEHOLD MAINTENANCE				
TAXES				
INSURANCE				
ELECTRICITY				
WATER				
SEWAGE				
GAS				
PHONE				
TRASH				
CABLE				
CELL PHONE				
GROCERIES				
ENTERTAINMENT				
CHARITY/DONATIONS				
FUEL				
AUTO INSURANCE				
CAR PAYMENT				
CHILD CARE				
CREDIT CARDS/DEBT				
LOANS				
DINING OUT				
SPORTING EVENTS				
LIVE THEATER				
CONCERTS				
MOVIES				
TOTAL EXPENSES				

NOTES

AUGUST

INCOMES & EXPENSES

DATE	INCOME	CATEGORY	AMOUNT
			TOTAL

DATE	EXPENSE	CATEGORY	AMOUNT
			TOTAL

AUGUST

INCOMES & EXPENSES

DATE	INCOME	CATEGORY	AMOUNT
			TOTAL

DATE	EXPENSE	CATEGORY	AMOUNT
			TOTAL

AUGUST

INCOMES & EXPENSES

DATE	INCOME	CATEGORY	AMOUNT
			TOTAL

DATE	EXPENSE	CATEGORY	AMOUNT
			TOTAL

AUGUST

INCOMES & EXPENSES

DATE	INCOME	CATEGORY	AMOUNT
			TOTAL

DATE	EXPENSE	CATEGORY	AMOUNT
			TOTAL

AUGUST

INCOMES & EXPENSES

DATE	INCOME	CATEGORY	AMOUNT
			TOTAL

DATE	EXPENSE	CATEGORY	AMOUNT
			TOTAL

MONTHLY BUDGET

MONTH OF

TOTAL INCOME

OTHER INCOME / SAVINGS

EXPENSES ITEM	BUDGET	ACTUAL	DIFFERENCE	NOTES
MORTGAGE/RENT				
HOUSEHOLD MAINTENANCE				
TAXES				
INSURANCE				
ELECTRICITY				
WATER				
SEWAGE				
GAS				
PHONE				
TRASH				
CABLE				
CELL PHONE				
GROCERIES				
ENTERTAINMENT				
CHARITY/DONATIONS				
FUEL				
AUTO INSURANCE				
CAR PAYMENT				
CHILD CARE				
CREDIT CARDS/DEBT				
LOANS				
DINING OUT				
SPORTING EVENTS				
LIVE THEATER				
CONCERTS				
MOVIES				
TOTAL EXPENSES				

NOTES

SEPTEMBER

INCOMES & EXPENSES

DATE	INCOME	CATEGORY	AMOUNT
			TOTAL

DATE	EXPENSE	CATEGORY	AMOUNT
			TOTAL

SEPTEMBER

INCOMES & EXPENSES

DATE	INCOME	CATEGORY	AMOUNT
			TOTAL

DATE	EXPENSE	CATEGORY	AMOUNT
			TOTAL

SEPTEMBER

INCOMES & EXPENSES

DATE	INCOME	CATEGORY	AMOUNT
			TOTAL

DATE	EXPENSE	CATEGORY	AMOUNT
			TOTAL

SEPTEMBER

INCOMES & EXPENSES

DATE	INCOME	CATEGORY	AMOUNT
			TOTAL

DATE	EXPENSE	CATEGORY	AMOUNT
			TOTAL

SEPTEMBER

INCOMES & EXPENSES

DATE	INCOME	CATEGORY	AMOUNT
			TOTAL

DATE	EXPENSE	CATEGORY	AMOUNT
			TOTAL

MONTHLY BUDGET

MONTH OF

TOTAL INCOME

OTHER INCOME / SAVINGS

EXPENSES ITEM	BUDGET	ACTUAL	DIFFERENCE	NOTES
MORTGAGE/RENT				
HOUSEHOLD MAINTENANCE				
TAXES				
INSURANCE				
ELECTRICITY				
WATER				
SEWAGE				
GAS				
PHONE				
TRASH				
CABLE				
CELL PHONE				
GROCERIES				
ENTERTAINMENT				
CHARITY/DONATIONS				
FUEL				
AUTO INSURANCE				
CAR PAYMENT				
CHILD CARE				
CREDIT CARDS/DEBT				
LOANS				
DINING OUT				
SPORTING EVENTS				
LIVE THEATER				
CONCERTS				
MOVIES				
TOTAL EXPENSES				

NOTES

OCTOBER

INCOMES & EXPENSES

DATE	INCOME	CATEGORY	AMOUNT
			TOTAL

DATE	EXPENSE	CATEGORY	AMOUNT
			TOTAL

OCTOBER

INCOMES & EXPENSES

DATE	INCOME	CATEGORY	AMOUNT
			TOTAL

DATE	EXPENSE	CATEGORY	AMOUNT
			TOTAL

OCTOBER

INCOMES & EXPENSES

DATE	INCOME	CATEGORY	AMOUNT
			TOTAL

DATE	EXPENSE	CATEGORY	AMOUNT
			TOTAL

OCTOBER

INCOMES & EXPENSES

DATE	INCOME	CATEGORY	AMOUNT
			TOTAL

DATE	EXPENSE	CATEGORY	AMOUNT
			TOTAL

OCTOBER

INCOMES & EXPENSES

DATE	INCOME	CATEGORY	AMOUNT
			TOTAL

DATE	EXPENSE	CATEGORY	AMOUNT
			TOTAL

MONTHLY BUDGET

MONTH OF	
TOTAL INCOME	OTHER INCOME / SAVINGS

EXPENSES ITEM	BUDGET	ACTUAL	DIFFERENCE	NOTES
MORTGAGE/RENT				
HOUSEHOLD MAINTENANCE				
TAXES				
INSURANCE				
ELECTRICITY				
WATER				
SEWAGE				
GAS				
PHONE				
TRASH				
CABLE				
CELL PHONE				
GROCERIES				
ENTERTAINMENT				
CHARITY/DONATIONS				
FUEL				
AUTO INSURANCE				
CAR PAYMENT				
CHILD CARE				
CREDIT CARDS/DEBT				
LOANS				
DINING OUT				
SPORTING EVENTS				
LIVE THEATER				
CONCERTS				
MOVIES				
TOTAL EXPENSES				

NOTES

NOVEMBER

INCOMES & EXPENSES

DATE	INCOME	CATEGORY	AMOUNT
			TOTAL

DATE	EXPENSE	CATEGORY	AMOUNT
			TOTAL

NOVEMBER

INCOMES & EXPENSES

DATE	INCOME	CATEGORY	AMOUNT
			TOTAL

DATE	EXPENSE	CATEGORY	AMOUNT
			TOTAL

NOVEMBER

INCOMES & EXPENSES

DATE	INCOME	CATEGORY	AMOUNT
			TOTAL

AMOUNT

DATE	EXPENSE	CATEGORY	
			TOTAL

NOVEMBER

INCOMES & EXPENSES

DATE	INCOME	CATEGORY	AMOUNT
			TOTAL

DATE	EXPENSE	CATEGORY	AMOUNT
			TOTAL

NOVEMBER

INCOMES & EXPENSES

DATE	INCOME	CATEGORY	AMOUNT
			TOTAL

DATE	EXPENSE	CATEGORY	AMOUNT
			TOTAL

MONTHLY BUDGET

MONTH OF

TOTAL INCOME

OTHER INCOME / SAVINGS

EXPENSES ITEM	BUDGET	ACTUAL	DIFFERENCE	NOTES
MORTGAGE/RENT				
HOUSEHOLD MAINTENANCE				
TAXES				
INSURANCE				
ELECTRICITY				
WATER				
SEWAGE				
GAS				
PHONE				
TRASH				
CABLE				
CELL PHONE				
GROCERIES				
ENTERTAINMENT				
CHARITY/DONATIONS				
FUEL				
AUTO INSURANCE				
CAR PAYMENT				
CHILD CARE				
CREDIT CARDS/DEBT				
LOANS				
DINING OUT				
SPORTING EVENTS				
LIVE THEATER				
CONCERTS				
MOVIES				
TOTAL EXPENSES				

NOTES

DECEMBER

INCOMES & EXPENSES

DATE	INCOME	CATEGORY	AMOUNT
			TOTAL

DATE	EXPENSE	CATEGORY	AMOUNT
			TOTAL

DECEMBER

INCOMES & EXPENSES

DATE	INCOME	CATEGORY	AMOUNT
			TOTAL

DATE	EXPENSE	CATEGORY	AMOUNT
			TOTAL

DECEMBER

INCOMES & EXPENSES

DATE	INCOME	CATEGORY	AMOUNT
			TOTAL

DATE	EXPENSE	CATEGORY	AMOUNT
			TOTAL

DECEMBER

INCOMES & EXPENSES

DATE	INCOME	CATEGORY	AMOUNT
			TOTAL

DATE	EXPENSE	CATEGORY	AMOUNT
			TOTAL

DECEMBER

INCOMES & EXPENSES

DATE	INCOME	CATEGORY	AMOUNT
			TOTAL

DATE	EXPENSE	CATEGORY	AMOUNT
			TOTAL

MONTHLY BUDGET

MONTH OF

TOTAL INCOME

OTHER INCOME / SAVINGS

EXPENSES ITEM	BUDGET	ACTUAL	DIFFERENCE	NOTES
MORTGAGE/RENT				
HOUSEHOLD MAINTENANCE				
TAXES				
INSURANCE				
ELECTRICITY				
WATER				
SEWAGE				
GAS				
PHONE				
TRASH				
CABLE				
CELL PHONE				
GROCERIES				
ENTERTAINMENT				
CHARITY/DONATIONS				
FUEL				
AUTO INSURANCE				
CAR PAYMENT				
CHILD CARE				
CREDIT CARDS/DEBT				
LOANS				
DINING OUT				
SPORTING EVENTS				
LIVE THEATER				
CONCERTS				
MOVIES				
TOTAL EXPENSES				

NOTES

JANUARY

INCOMES & EXPENSES

DATE	INCOME	CATEGORY	AMOUNT
		TOTAL	

DATE	EXPENSE	CATEGORY	AMOUNT
		TOTAL	

JANUARY

INCOMES & EXPENSES

DATE	INCOME	CATEGORY	AMOUNT
			TOTAL

DATE	EXPENSE	CATEGORY	AMOUNT
			TOTAL

JANUARY

INCOMES & EXPENSES

DATE	INCOME	CATEGORY	AMOUNT
			TOTAL

DATE	EXPENSE	CATEGORY	AMOUNT
			TOTAL

JANUARY

INCOMES & EXPENSES

DATE	INCOME	CATEGORY	AMOUNT
			TOTAL

DATE	EXPENSE	CATEGORY	AMOUNT
			TOTAL

JANUARY

INCOMES & EXPENSES

DATE	INCOME	CATEGORY	AMOUNT
			TOTAL

DATE	EXPENSE	CATEGORY	AMOUNT
			TOTAL

MONTHLY BUDGET

MONTH OF				
TOTAL INCOME		OTHER INCOME / SAVINGS		

EXPENSES ITEM	BUDGET	ACTUAL	DIFFERENCE	NOTES
MORTGAGE/RENT				
HOUSEHOLD MAINTENANCE				
TAXES				
INSURANCE				
ELECTRICITY				
WATER				
SEWAGE				
GAS				
PHONE				
TRASH				
CABLE				
CELL PHONE				
GROCERIES				
ENTERTAINMENT				
CHARITY/DONATIONS				
FUEL				
AUTO INSURANCE				
CAR PAYMENT				
CHILD CARE				
CREDIT CARDS/DEBT				
LOANS				
DINING OUT				
SPORTING EVENTS				
LIVE THEATER				
CONCERTS				
MOVIES				
TOTAL EXPENSES				

NOTES

FEBRUARY

INCOMES & EXPENSES

DATE	INCOME	CATEGORY	AMOUNT
			TOTAL

DATE	EXPENSE	CATEGORY	AMOUNT
			TOTAL

FEBRUARY

INCOMES & EXPENSES

DATE	INCOME	CATEGORY	AMOUNT
			TOTAL

DATE	EXPENSE	CATEGORY	AMOUNT
			TOTAL

FEBRUARY

INCOMES & EXPENSES

DATE	INCOME	CATEGORY	AMOUNT
			TOTAL

DATE	EXPENSE	CATEGORY	AMOUNT
			TOTAL

FEBRUARY

INCOMES & EXPENSES

DATE	INCOME	CATEGORY	AMOUNT
			TOTAL

DATE	EXPENSE	CATEGORY	AMOUNT
			TOTAL

FEBRUARY

INCOMES & EXPENSES

DATE	INCOME	CATEGORY	AMOUNT
			TOTAL

DATE	EXPENSE	CATEGORY	AMOUNT
			TOTAL

MONTHLY BUDGET

MONTH OF	
TOTAL INCOME	OTHER INCOME / SAVINGS

EXPENSES ITEM	BUDGET	ACTUAL	DIFFERENCE	NOTES
MORTGAGE/RENT				
HOUSEHOLD MAINTENANCE				
TAXES				
INSURANCE				
ELECTRICITY				
WATER				
SEWAGE				
GAS				
PHONE				
TRASH				
CABLE				
CELL PHONE				
GROCERIES				
ENTERTAINMENT				
CHARITY/DONATIONS				
FUEL				
AUTO INSURANCE				
CAR PAYMENT				
CHILD CARE				
CREDIT CARDS/DEBT				
LOANS				
DINING OUT				
SPORTING EVENTS				
LIVE THEATER				
CONCERTS				
MOVIES				
TOTAL EXPENSES				

NOTES

MARCH

INCOMES & EXPENSES

DATE	INCOME	CATEGORY	AMOUNT
		TOTAL	

DATE	EXPENSE	CATEGORY	AMOUNT
		TOTAL	

MARCH

INCOMES & EXPENSES

DATE	INCOME	CATEGORY	AMOUNT
			TOTAL

DATE	EXPENSE	CATEGORY	AMOUNT
			TOTAL

MARCH

INCOMES & EXPENSES

DATE	INCOME	CATEGORY	AMOUNT
			TOTAL

DATE	EXPENSE	CATEGORY	AMOUNT
			TOTAL

MARCH

INCOMES & EXPENSES

DATE	INCOME	CATEGORY	AMOUNT
			TOTAL

DATE	EXPENSE	CATEGORY	AMOUNT
			TOTAL

MARCH

INCOMES & EXPENSES

DATE	INCOME	CATEGORY	AMOUNT
		TOTAL	

DATE	EXPENSE	CATEGORY	AMOUNT
		TOTAL	

MARCH

INCOMES & EXPENSES

DATE	INCOME	CATEGORY	AMOUNT
			TOTAL

DATE	EXPENSE	CATEGORY	AMOUNT
			TOTAL

APRIL

INCOMES & EXPENSES

DATE	INCOME	CATEGORY	AMOUNT
			TOTAL

DATE	EXPENSE	CATEGORY	AMOUNT
			TOTAL

MONTHLY BUDGET

MONTH OF

TOTAL INCOME | OTHER INCOME / SAVINGS

EXPENSES ITEM	BUDGET	ACTUAL	DIFFERENCE	NOTES
MORTGAGE/RENT				
HOUSEHOLD MAINTENANCE				
TAXES				
INSURANCE				
ELECTRICITY				
WATER				
SEWAGE				
GAS				
PHONE				
TRASH				
CABLE				
CELL PHONE				
GROCERIES				
ENTERTAINMENT				
CHARITY/DONATIONS				
FUEL				
AUTO INSURANCE				
CAR PAYMENT				
CHILD CARE				
CREDIT CARDS/DEBT				
LOANS				
DINING OUT				
SPORTING EVENTS				
LIVE THEATER				
CONCERTS				
MOVIES				
TOTAL EXPENSES				

NOTES

APRIL

INCOMES & EXPENSES

DATE	INCOME	CATEGORY	AMOUNT
			TOTAL

DATE	EXPENSE	CATEGORY	AMOUNT
			TOTAL

APRIL

INCOMES & EXPENSES

DATE	INCOME	CATEGORY	AMOUNT
			TOTAL

DATE	EXPENSE	CATEGORY	AMOUNT
			TOTAL

APRIL

INCOMES & EXPENSES

DATE	INCOME	CATEGORY	AMOUNT
			TOTAL

DATE	EXPENSE	CATEGORY	AMOUNT
			TOTAL

APRIL

INCOMES & EXPENSES

DATE	INCOME	CATEGORY	AMOUNT
			TOTAL

DATE	EXPENSE	CATEGORY	AMOUNT
			TOTAL

APRIL

INCOMES & EXPENSES

DATE	INCOME	CATEGORY	AMOUNT
			TOTAL

DATE	EXPENSE	CATEGORY	AMOUNT
			TOTAL

MONTHLY BUDGET

MONTH OF

TOTAL INCOME	OTHER INCOME / SAVINGS

EXPENSES ITEM	BUDGET	ACTUAL	DIFFERENCE	NOTES
MORTGAGE/RENT				
HOUSEHOLD MAINTENANCE				
TAXES				
INSURANCE				
ELECTRICITY				
WATER				
SEWAGE				
GAS				
PHONE				
TRASH				
CABLE				
CELL PHONE				
GROCERIES				
ENTERTAINMENT				
CHARITY/DONATIONS				
FUEL				
AUTO INSURANCE				
CAR PAYMENT				
CHILD CARE				
CREDIT CARDS/DEBT				
LOANS				
DINING OUT				
SPORTING EVENTS				
LIVE THEATER				
CONCERTS				
MOVIES				
TOTAL EXPENSES				

NOTES

MAY

INCOMES & EXPENSES

DATE	INCOME	CATEGORY	AMOUNT
			TOTAL

DATE	EXPENSE	CATEGORY	AMOUNT
			TOTAL

MAY

INCOMES & EXPENSES

DATE	INCOME	CATEGORY	AMOUNT
			TOTAL

DATE	EXPENSE	CATEGORY	AMOUNT
			TOTAL

MAY

INCOMES & EXPENSES

DATE	INCOME	CATEGORY	AMOUNT
			TOTAL

DATE	EXPENSE	CATEGORY	AMOUNT
			TOTAL

MAY

INCOMES & EXPENSES

DATE	INCOME	CATEGORY	AMOUNT
			TOTAL

DATE	EXPENSE	CATEGORY	AMOUNT
			TOTAL

MAY

INCOMES & EXPENSES

DATE	INCOME	CATEGORY	AMOUNT
			TOTAL

DATE	EXPENSE	CATEGORY	AMOUNT
			TOTAL

MONTHLY BUDGET

MONTH OF	
TOTAL INCOME	OTHER INCOME / SAVINGS

EXPENSES ITEM	BUDGET	ACTUAL	DIFFERENCE	NOTES
MORTGAGE/RENT				
HOUSEHOLD MAINTENANCE				
TAXES				
INSURANCE				
ELECTRICITY				
WATER				
SEWAGE				
GAS				
PHONE				
TRASH				
CABLE				
CELL PHONE				
GROCERIES				
ENTERTAINMENT				
CHARITY/DONATIONS				
FUEL				
AUTO INSURANCE				
CAR PAYMENT				
CHILD CARE				
CREDIT CARDS/DEBT				
LOANS				
DINING OUT				
SPORTING EVENTS				
LIVE THEATER				
CONCERTS				
MOVIES				
TOTAL EXPENSES				

NOTES

JUNE

INCOMES & EXPENSES

DATE	INCOME	CATEGORY	AMOUNT
			TOTAL

DATE	EXPENSE	CATEGORY	AMOUNT
			TOTAL

JUNE

INCOMES & EXPENSES

DATE	INCOME	CATEGORY	AMOUNT
			TOTAL

DATE	EXPENSE	CATEGORY	AMOUNT
			TOTAL

JUNE

INCOMES & EXPENSES

DATE	INCOME	CATEGORY	AMOUNT
			TOTAL

DATE	EXPENSE	CATEGORY	AMOUNT
			TOTAL

JUNE

INCOMES & EXPENSES

DATE	INCOME	CATEGORY	AMOUNT
			TOTAL

DATE	EXPENSE	CATEGORY	AMOUNT
			TOTAL

JUNE

INCOMES & EXPENSES

DATE	INCOME	CATEGORY	AMOUNT
			TOTAL

DATE	EXPENSE	CATEGORY	AMOUNT
			TOTAL

MONTHLY BUDGET

MONTH OF	
TOTAL INCOME	OTHER INCOME / SAVINGS

EXPENSES ITEM	BUDGET	ACTUAL	DIFFERENCE	NOTES
MORTGAGE/RENT				
HOUSEHOLD MAINTENANCE				
TAXES				
INSURANCE				
ELECTRICITY				
WATER				
SEWAGE				
GAS				
PHONE				
TRASH				
CABLE				
CELL PHONE				
GROCERIES				
ENTERTAINMENT				
CHARITY/DONATIONS				
FUEL				
AUTO INSURANCE				
CAR PAYMENT				
CHILD CARE				
CREDIT CARDS/DEBT				
LOANS				
DINING OUT				
SPORTING EVENTS				
LIVE THEATER				
CONCERTS				
MOVIES				
TOTAL EXPENSES				

NOTES

JULY

INCOMES & EXPENSES

DATE	INCOME	CATEGORY	AMOUNT
		TOTAL	

DATE	EXPENSE	CATEGORY	AMOUNT
		TOTAL	

JULY

INCOMES & EXPENSES

DATE	INCOME	CATEGORY	AMOUNT
			TOTAL

DATE	EXPENSE	CATEGORY	AMOUNT
			TOTAL

JULY

INCOMES & EXPENSES

DATE	INCOME	CATEGORY	AMOUNT
			TOTAL

DATE	EXPENSE	CATEGORY	AMOUNT
			TOTAL

JULY

INCOMES & EXPENSES

DATE	INCOME	CATEGORY	AMOUNT
			TOTAL

DATE	EXPENSE	CATEGORY	AMOUNT
			TOTAL

JULY

INCOMES & EXPENSES

DATE	INCOME	CATEGORY	AMOUNT
			TOTAL

DATE	EXPENSE	CATEGORY	AMOUNT
			TOTAL

MONTHLY BUDGET

MONTH OF

TOTAL INCOME

OTHER INCOME / SAVINGS

EXPENSES ITEM	BUDGET	ACTUAL	DIFFERENCE	NOTES
MORTGAGE/RENT				
HOUSEHOLD MAINTENANCE				
TAXES				
INSURANCE				
ELECTRICITY				
WATER				
SEWAGE				
GAS				
PHONE				
TRASH				
CABLE				
CELL PHONE				
GROCERIES				
ENTERTAINMENT				
CHARITY/DONATIONS				
FUEL				
AUTO INSURANCE				
CAR PAYMENT				
CHILD CARE				
CREDIT CARDS/DEBT				
LOANS				
DINING OUT				
SPORTING EVENTS				
LIVE THEATER				
CONCERTS				
MOVIES				
TOTAL EXPENSES				

NOTES

AUGUST

INCOMES & EXPENSES

DATE	INCOME	CATEGORY	AMOUNT
			TOTAL

DATE	EXPENSE	CATEGORY	AMOUNT
			TOTAL

AUGUST

INCOMES & EXPENSES

DATE	INCOME	CATEGORY	AMOUNT
			TOTAL

DATE	EXPENSE	CATEGORY	AMOUNT
			TOTAL

AUGUST

INCOMES & EXPENSES

DATE	INCOME	CATEGORY	AMOUNT
			TOTAL

DATE	EXPENSE	CATEGORY	AMOUNT
			TOTAL

AUGUST

INCOMES & EXPENSES

DATE	INCOME	CATEGORY	AMOUNT
			TOTAL

DATE	EXPENSE	CATEGORY	AMOUNT
			TOTAL

AUGUST

INCOMES & EXPENSES

DATE	INCOME	CATEGORY	AMOUNT
			TOTAL

DATE	EXPENSE	CATEGORY	AMOUNT
			TOTAL

MONTHLY BUDGET

MONTH OF				
TOTAL INCOME		OTHER INCOME / SAVINGS		

EXPENSES ITEM	BUDGET	ACTUAL	DIFFERENCE	NOTES
MORTGAGE/RENT				
HOUSEHOLD MAINTENANCE				
TAXES				
INSURANCE				
ELECTRICITY				
WATER				
SEWAGE				
GAS				
PHONE				
TRASH				
CABLE				
CELL PHONE				
GROCERIES				
ENTERTAINMENT				
CHARITY/DONATIONS				
FUEL				
AUTO INSURANCE				
CAR PAYMENT				
CHILD CARE				
CREDIT CARDS/DEBT				
LOANS				
DINING OUT				
SPORTING EVENTS				
LIVE THEATER				
CONCERTS				
MOVIES				
TOTAL EXPENSES				

NOTES

SEPTEMBER

INCOMES & EXPENSES

DATE	INCOME	CATEGORY	AMOUNT
			TOTAL

DATE	EXPENSE	CATEGORY	AMOUNT
			TOTAL

SEPTEMBER

INCOMES & EXPENSES

DATE	INCOME	CATEGORY	AMOUNT
			TOTAL

DATE	EXPENSE	CATEGORY	AMOUNT
			TOTAL

SEPTEMBER

INCOMES & EXPENSES

DATE	INCOME	CATEGORY	AMOUNT
			TOTAL

DATE	EXPENSE	CATEGORY	AMOUNT
			TOTAL

SEPTEMBER

INCOMES & EXPENSES

DATE	INCOME	CATEGORY	AMOUNT
			TOTAL

DATE	EXPENSE	CATEGORY	AMOUNT
			TOTAL

SEPTEMBER

INCOMES & EXPENSES

DATE	INCOME	CATEGORY	AMOUNT
			TOTAL

DATE	EXPENSE	CATEGORY	AMOUNT
			TOTAL

MONTHLY BUDGET

MONTH OF	
TOTAL INCOME	OTHER INCOME / SAVINGS

EXPENSES ITEM	BUDGET	ACTUAL	DIFFERENCE	NOTES
MORTGAGE/RENT				
HOUSEHOLD MAINTENANCE				
TAXES				
INSURANCE				
ELECTRICITY				
WATER				
SEWAGE				
GAS				
PHONE				
TRASH				
CABLE				
CELL PHONE				
GROCERIES				
ENTERTAINMENT				
CHARITY/DONATIONS				
FUEL				
AUTO INSURANCE				
CAR PAYMENT				
CHILD CARE				
CREDIT CARDS/DEBT				
LOANS				
DINING OUT				
SPORTING EVENTS				
LIVE THEATER				
CONCERTS				
MOVIES				
TOTAL EXPENSES				

NOTES

OCTOBER

INCOMES & EXPENSES

DATE	INCOME	CATEGORY	AMOUNT
			TOTAL

DATE	EXPENSE	CATEGORY	AMOUNT
			TOTAL

OCTOBER

INCOMES & EXPENSES

DATE	INCOME	CATEGORY	AMOUNT
			TOTAL

DATE	EXPENSE	CATEGORY	AMOUNT
			TOTAL

OCTOBER

INCOMES & EXPENSES

DATE	INCOME	CATEGORY	AMOUNT
			TOTAL

DATE	EXPENSE	CATEGORY	AMOUNT
			TOTAL

OCTOBER

INCOMES & EXPENSES

DATE	INCOME	CATEGORY	AMOUNT
			TOTAL

DATE	EXPENSE	CATEGORY	AMOUNT
			TOTAL

OCTOBER

INCOMES & EXPENSES

DATE	INCOME	CATEGORY	AMOUNT
			TOTAL

DATE	EXPENSE	CATEGORY	AMOUNT
			TOTAL

MONTHLY BUDGET

MONTH OF

TOTAL INCOME

OTHER INCOME / SAVINGS

EXPENSES ITEM	BUDGET	ACTUAL	DIFFERENCE	NOTES
MORTGAGE/RENT				
HOUSEHOLD MAINTENANCE				
TAXES				
INSURANCE				
ELECTRICITY				
WATER				
SEWAGE				
GAS				
PHONE				
TRASH				
CABLE				
CELL PHONE				
GROCERIES				
ENTERTAINMENT				
CHARITY/DONATIONS				
FUEL				
AUTO INSURANCE				
CAR PAYMENT				
CHILD CARE				
CREDIT CARDS/DEBT				
LOANS				
DINING OUT				
SPORTING EVENTS				
LIVE THEATER				
CONCERTS				
MOVIES				
TOTAL EXPENSES				

NOTES

NOVEMBER

INCOMES & EXPENSES

DATE	INCOME	CATEGORY	AMOUNT
			TOTAL

DATE	EXPENSE	CATEGORY	AMOUNT
			TOTAL

NOVEMBER

INCOMES & EXPENSES

DATE	INCOME	CATEGORY	AMOUNT
			TOTAL

DATE	EXPENSE	CATEGORY	AMOUNT
			TOTAL

NOVEMBER

INCOMES & EXPENSES

DATE	INCOME	CATEGORY	AMOUNT
			TOTAL

DATE	EXPENSE	CATEGORY	AMOUNT
			TOTAL

NOVEMBER

INCOMES & EXPENSES

DATE	INCOME	CATEGORY	AMOUNT
			TOTAL

DATE	EXPENSE	CATEGORY	AMOUNT
			TOTAL

NOVEMBER

INCOMES & EXPENSES

DATE	INCOME	CATEGORY	AMOUNT
			TOTAL

DATE	EXPENSE	CATEGORY	AMOUNT
			TOTAL

MONTHLY BUDGET

MONTH OF

TOTAL INCOME

OTHER INCOME / SAVINGS

EXPENSES ITEM	BUDGET	ACTUAL	DIFFERENCE	NOTES
MORTGAGE/RENT				
HOUSEHOLD MAINTENANCE				
TAXES				
INSURANCE				
ELECTRICITY				
WATER				
SEWAGE				
GAS				
PHONE				
TRASH				
CABLE				
CELL PHONE				
GROCERIES				
ENTERTAINMENT				
CHARITY/DONATIONS				
FUEL				
AUTO INSURANCE				
CAR PAYMENT				
CHILD CARE				
CREDIT CARDS/DEBT				
LOANS				
DINING OUT				
SPORTING EVENTS				
LIVE THEATER				
CONCERTS				
MOVIES				
TOTAL EXPENSES				

NOTES

DECEMBER

INCOMES & EXPENSES

DATE	INCOME	CATEGORY	AMOUNT
			TOTAL

DATE	EXPENSE	CATEGORY	AMOUNT
			TOTAL

DECEMBER

INCOMES & EXPENSES

DATE	INCOME	CATEGORY	AMOUNT
			TOTAL

DATE	EXPENSE	CATEGORY	AMOUNT
			TOTAL

DECEMBER

INCOMES & EXPENSES

DATE	INCOME	CATEGORY	AMOUNT
			TOTAL

DATE	EXPENSE	CATEGORY	AMOUNT
			TOTAL

DECEMBER

INCOMES & EXPENSES

DATE	INCOME	CATEGORY	AMOUNT
			TOTAL

DATE	EXPENSE	CATEGORY	AMOUNT
			TOTAL

DECEMBER

INCOMES & EXPENSES

DATE	INCOME	CATEGORY	AMOUNT
		TOTAL	

DATE	EXPENSE	CATEGORY	AMOUNT
		TOTAL	

MONTHLY BUDGET

MONTH OF

TOTAL INCOME | OTHER INCOME / SAVINGS

EXPENSES ITEM	BUDGET	ACTUAL	DIFFERENCE	NOTES
MORTGAGE/RENT				
HOUSEHOLD MAINTENANCE				
TAXES				
INSURANCE				
ELECTRICITY				
WATER				
SEWAGE				
GAS				
PHONE				
TRASH				
CABLE				
CELL PHONE				
GROCERIES				
ENTERTAINMENT				
CHARITY/DONATIONS				
FUEL				
AUTO INSURANCE				
CAR PAYMENT				
CHILD CARE				
CREDIT CARDS/DEBT				
LOANS				
DINING OUT				
SPORTING EVENTS				
LIVE THEATER				
CONCERTS				
MOVIES				
TOTAL EXPENSES				

NOTES

WHICH DEBT TRACKING METHOD IS RIGHT FOR YOU?

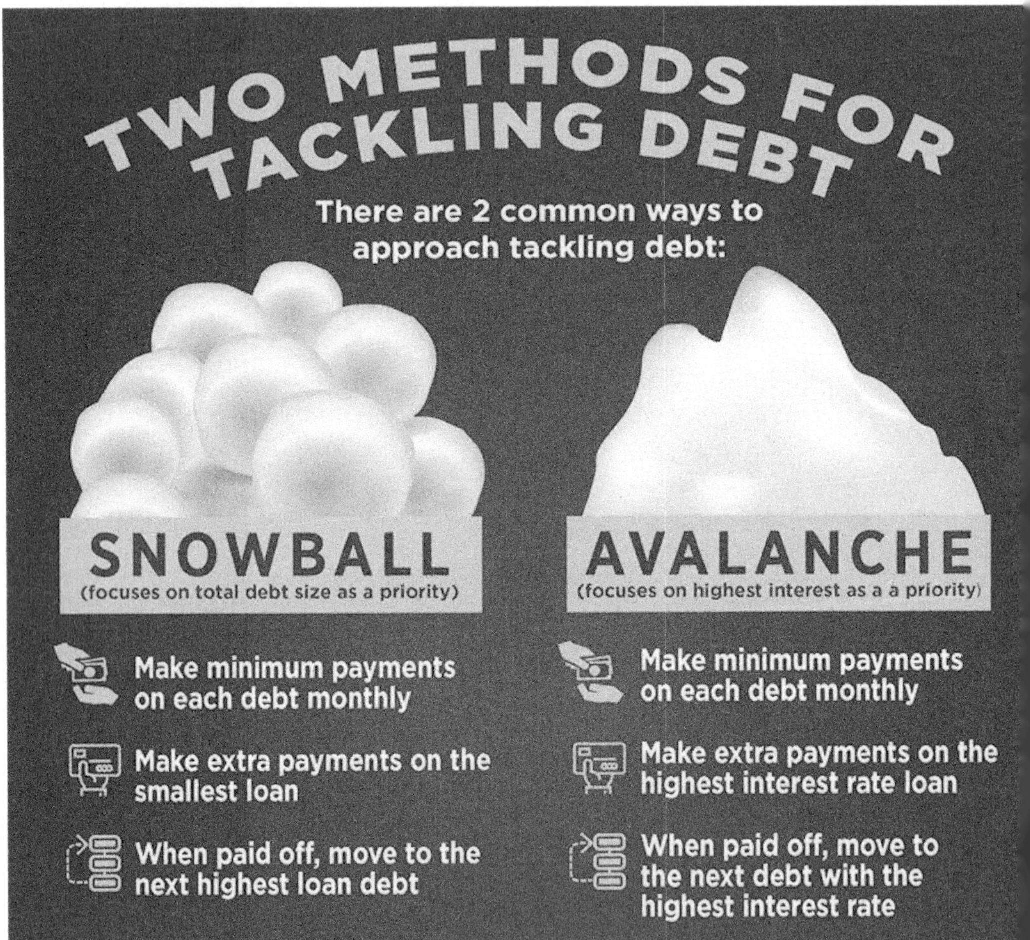

FOR ADDITIONAL HELP, RESOURCES, AND COMPLETE GUIDES ON DEBT RELIEF AND FINANCIAL PLANNING

GO TO

DEBTREDUCTION101.COM

DEBT TRACKER

Debt :

Balance :

Min. Payment :

DATE	PAYMENT	BALANCE

Debt :

Balance :

Min. Payment :

DATE	PAYMENT	BALANCE

Debt :

Balance :

Min. Payment :

DATE	PAYMENT	BALANCE

Debt :

Balance :

Min. Payment :

DATE	PAYMENT	BALANCE

DEBT TRACKER

Debt :

Balance :

Min. Payment :

DATE	PAYMENT	BALANCE

Debt :

Balance :

Min. Payment :

DATE	PAYMENT	BALANCE

Debt :

Balance :

Min. Payment :

DATE	PAYMENT	BALANCE

Debt :

Balance :

Min. Payment :

DATE	PAYMENT	BALANCE

DEBT TRACKER

Debt :

Balance :

Min. Payment :

DATE	PAYMENT	BALANCE

Debt :

Balance :

Min. Payment :

DATE	PAYMENT	BALANCE

Debt :

Balance :

Min. Payment :

DATE	PAYMENT	BALANCE

Debt :

Balance :

Min. Payment :

DATE	PAYMENT	BALANCE

DEBT TRACKER

Debt :

Balance :

Min. Payment :

DATE	PAYMENT	BALANCE

Debt :

Balance :

Min. Payment :

DATE	PAYMENT	BALANCE

Debt :

Balance :

Min. Payment :

DATE	PAYMENT	BALANCE

Debt :

Balance :

Min. Payment :

DATE	PAYMENT	BALANCE

DEBT TRACKER

Debt :

Balance :

Min. Payment :

DATE	PAYMENT	BALANCE

Debt :

Balance :

Min. Payment :

DATE	PAYMENT	BALANCE

Debt :

Balance :

Min. Payment :

DATE	PAYMENT	BALANCE

Debt :

Balance :

Min. Payment :

DATE	PAYMENT	BALANCE

DEBT TRACKER

Debt :

Balance :

Min. Payment :

DATE	PAYMENT	BALANCE

Debt :

Balance :

Min. Payment :

DATE	PAYMENT	BALANCE

Debt :

Balance :

Min. Payment :

DATE	PAYMENT	BALANCE

Debt :

Balance :

Min. Payment :

DATE	PAYMENT	BALANCE

NOTES

DEBT SNOWBALL TRACKER

DATE RANGE

CREDITOR

ACCOUNT #

AMOUNT

DUE DATE

INTEREST RATE

GOAL PAYOFF DATE

MINIMUM PAYMENT

DATE	ACCOUNT	BALANCE	NOTES

VISUAL PAYOFF PROGRESS

$ 100%
$ 95%
$ 90%
$ 85%
$ 80%
$ 75%
$ 70%
$ 65%
$ 60%
$ 55%
$ 50%
$ 45%
$ 40%
$ 35%
$ 30%
$ 25%
$ 20%
$ 15%
$ 10%
$ 5%
$ 0%

DEBT SNOWBALL TRACKER

DATE RANGE

CREDITOR

ACCOUNT #

AMOUNT

DUE DATE

INTEREST RATE

GOAL PAYOFF DATE

MINIMUM PAYMENT

DATE	ACCOUNT	BALANCE	NOTES

VISUAL PAYOFF PROGRESS

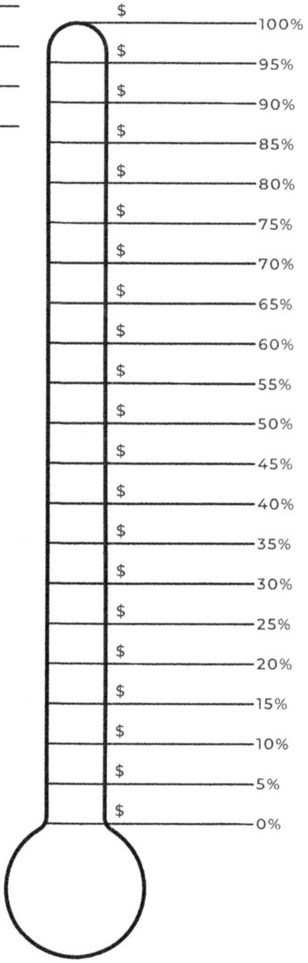

DEBT SNOWBALL TRACKER

DATE RANGE

CREDITOR

ACCOUNT #

AMOUNT

DUE DATE

INTEREST RATE

GOAL PAYOFF DATE

MINIMUM PAYMENT

DATE	ACCOUNT	BALANCE	NOTES

VISUAL PAYOFF PROGRESS

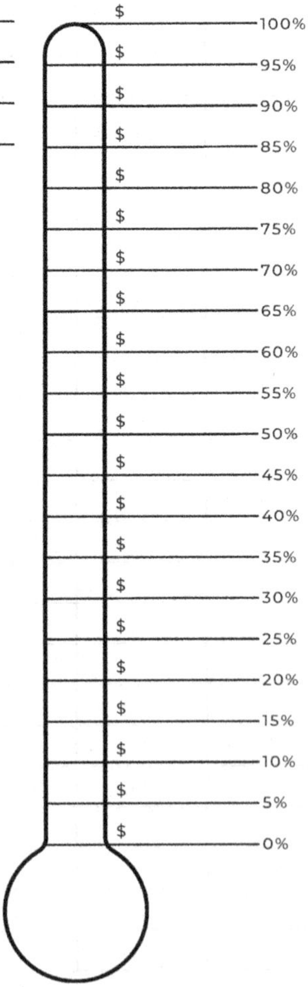

DEBT SNOWBALL TRACKER

DATE RANGE

CREDITOR

ACCOUNT #

AMOUNT

DUE DATE

INTEREST RATE

GOAL PAYOFF DATE

MINIMUM PAYMENT

DATE	ACCOUNT	BALANCE	NOTES

VISUAL PAYOFF PROGRESS

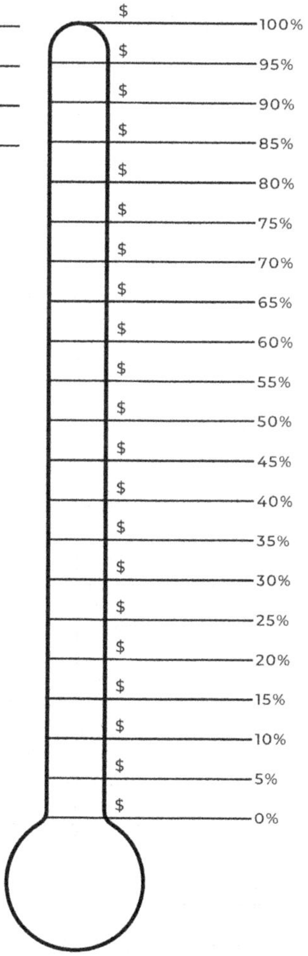

DEBT SNOWBALL TRACKER

DATE RANGE

CREDITOR

ACCOUNT #

AMOUNT

DUE DATE

INTEREST RATE

GOAL PAYOFF DATE

MINIMUM PAYMENT

DATE	ACCOUNT	BALANCE	NOTES

VISUAL PAYOFF PROGRESS

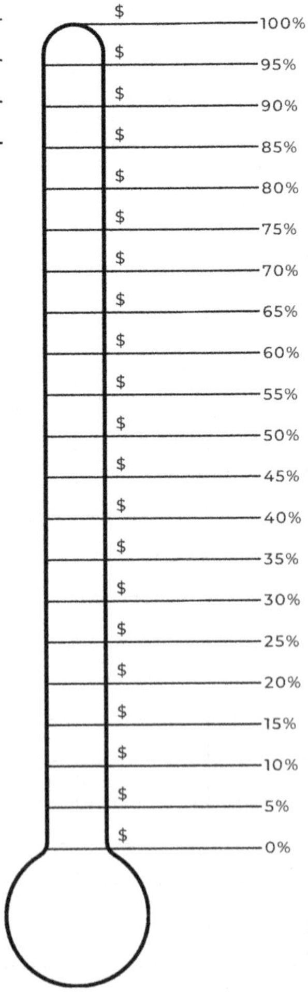

DEBT SNOWBALL TRACKER

DATE RANGE

CREDITOR

ACCOUNT #

AMOUNT

DUE DATE

INTEREST RATE

GOAL PAYOFF DATE

MINIMUM PAYMENT

DATE	ACCOUNT	BALANCE	NOTES

VISUAL PAYOFF PROGRESS

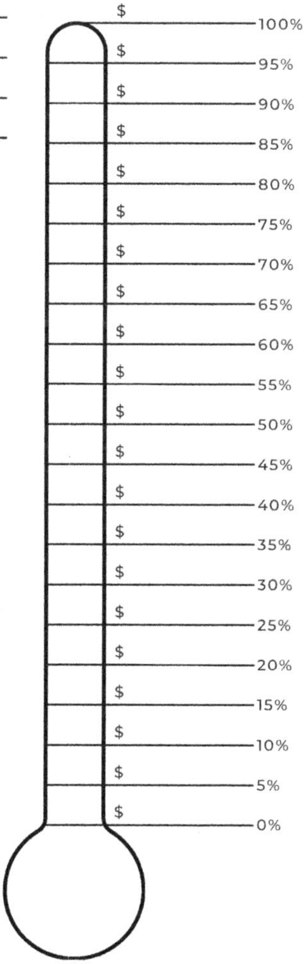

DEBT SNOWBALL TRACKER

DATE RANGE

CREDITOR | ACCOUNT #

AMOUNT | DUE DATE | INTEREST RATE

GOAL PAYOFF DATE | MINIMUM PAYMENT

DATE	ACCOUNT	BALANCE	NOTES

VISUAL PAYOFF PROGRESS

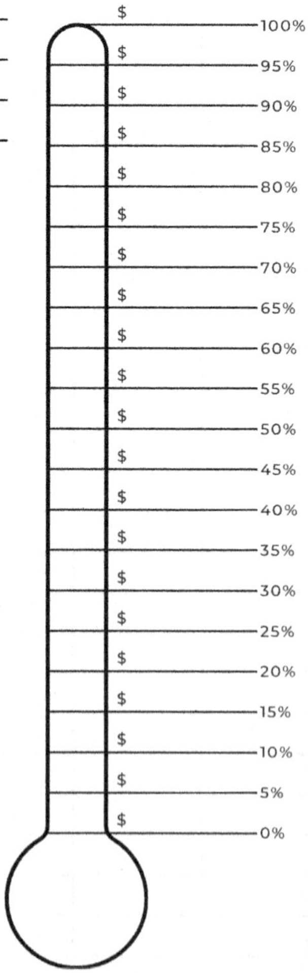

DEBT SNOWBALL TRACKER

DATE RANGE

CREDITOR

ACCOUNT #

AMOUNT

DUE DATE

INTEREST RATE

GOAL PAYOFF DATE

MINIMUM PAYMENT

DATE	ACCOUNT	BALANCE	NOTES

VISUAL PAYOFF PROGRESS

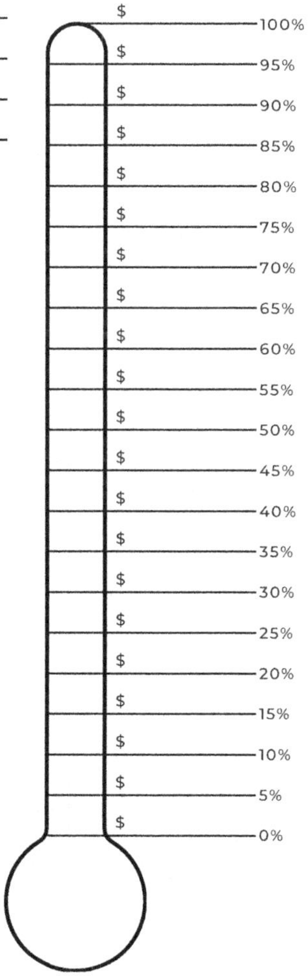

DEBT SNOWBALL TRACKER

DATE RANGE

CREDITOR

ACCOUNT #

AMOUNT

DUE DATE

INTEREST RATE

GOAL PAYOFF DATE

MINIMUM PAYMENT

DATE	ACCOUNT	BALANCE	NOTES

VISUAL PAYOFF PROGRESS

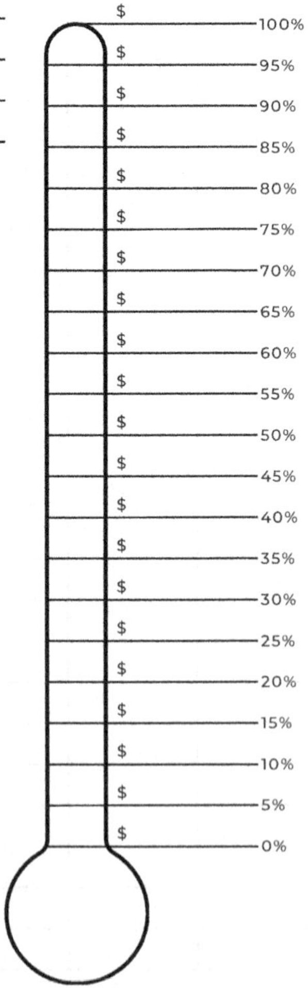

FOR ADDITIONAL HELP, RESOURCES, AND COMPLE GUIDES ON DEBT RELIEF AND FINANCIAL PLANNIN

GO TO

DEBTREDUCTION101.COM

T E

G

Made in the USA
Monee, IL
04 November 2026

67375791R00125